SUCCESS

Communicating in English

Michael Walker

Textbook

BASIC BEGINNER LEVEL

Addison-Wesley Publishing Company, World Language Division

Reading, Massachusetts · Menlo Park, California · New York
Don Mills, Ontario · Wokingham, England · Amsterdam · Bonn
Sydney · Singapore · Tokyo · Madrid · San Juan · Paris
Seoul, Korea · Milan · Mexico City · Taipei, Taiwan

ISBN: 0-201-59590-7
2 3 4 5 6 7 8 9 10 BAM 98 97 96 95

CONTENTS

 START WITH HELLO 4
AND GOOD-BYE

Introductions · Greetings and Leavetakings

1 THE TRAIN STATION 6

Numbers 1-10 · Greetings and introductions
Articles of clothing (singular) · Asking and
answering simple questions

To be: *is/isn't* · Possessive pronouns: *my/your
his/her* · Demonstratives: *this/that*

Skills Check 16

2 THE CLOTHING STORE 18

Articles of clothing (plural) · Colors · Numbers
(11-20)

Present progressive · To be: *is/are*

Skills Check 28

3 AT HOME 30

Household rooms/Furnishings · Taking public
transportation · Telling time

Prepositions: *in/on/at/under*

Skills Check 40

4 AT THE OFFICE 42

Office locations/Furnishings · Family members
Money · Making phone calls · Giving name and
address · Descriptive adjectives

Question words: *who/what/where* · Present
progressive

Skills Check 52

IN THE KITCHEN 54

Kitchen vocabulary · Food · Arranging to meet
Community locations

Articles: *a/an* · Questions and answers in present
progressive

Skills Check 64

THE COMMUNITY CENTER 66

Occupations · Looking for a job · Discussing
nationalities · Dealing with an emergency
Reading for information · Getting information
from advertisements

Question words: *How many?* · *There is/
There are*

Skills Check 76

FAMILY REUNION 78

Park and recreation activities · Family members ·
Ages · Health and feelings · Parts of the body ·
Describing location and ongoing activities · Giving
directions

Action verbs, Present progressive · Question
words: *who/what/where/which*

Skills Check 88

ON THE PHONE 90

Community locations · Asking for and giving
directions · Inquiring about a job · Reading and
responding to classified ads · Days of the week ·
Months of the year · Weather vocabulary

Prepositions: *next to/behind/on the left/on the
right*

Skills Check 100

GRAMMAR SUMMARY 102

INDEX 103

These pages highlight major themes, language functions, and forms. See the Teacher Resource Book for a
complete Scope and Sequence and information about all the *SUCCESS* components.

HELLO AND GOODBYE

Listen first. Practice the conversations.

1

2

Greetings
Introducing people

Good morning, Tom.
    Good morning, Mary. Is his name **John Romer?**
No, it is not.
    Well, what is it?
It is **John Hall.**

Make new conversations.

1. Is his name Frank Jones?   No, it is not.
    Well, what is it?   It is Frank Simon.

Frank Simon

2. Is her name Sally Siska?   No, it is not.
    Well, what is it?   It is Sally Clark.

Sally Clark

Listen first. Practice the model conversations.

1.

Hi, what's your name?

My name is **Tom West.**

My name is **Mary Brown.**
What's *your* name?

2.

What's her name?

Her name is **Karen.**

3.

Karen, this is a new
student, Tom West.

Hello, Tom. Pleased
to meet you.

Hello, Karen.
Glad to meet *you.*
What's your last name, Karen?

It's **Nelson.**

Greetings and introductions
Roleplaying conversations

10

4.

5.

Listen first. Practice the model conversations.
Make new conversations.

What is this?

It is a **hat.**

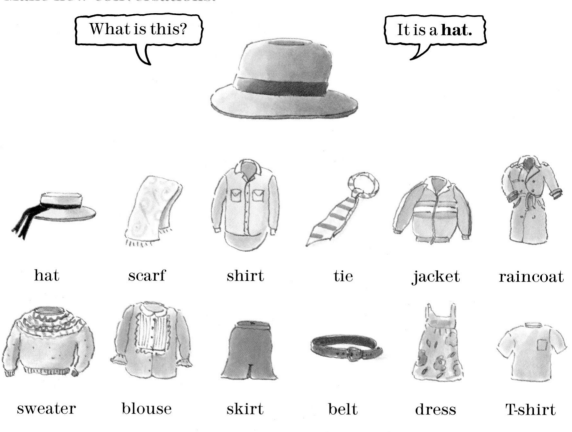

| hat | scarf | shirt | tie | jacket | raincoat |

| sweater | blouse | skirt | belt | dress | T-shirt |

Is this a **tie?**

Well, what is it?

No, it is not.

It is a **scarf.**

1.

2.

3.

4.

Identifying clothing (singular)
Question word: *what*

Listen first. Practice the model sentences. Make new sentences.

This is **her sweater.**

That is **her scarf.**

This is **his shirt.**

That is **his tie.**

1.

2.

3.

4.

Listen first. Practice the model conversations.

Excuse me. Is your last name Miller?

Is this your **hat**?

Here you are.

You're welcome.

Yes, it is.

Yes, it is.

Thank you. I forget everything!

Excuse me. Is this your **purse**?

Oh, sorry.

No, it isn't.

No problem.

Identifying personal belongings
Roleplaying conversations

14

Useful Words

Listen first. Then listen again and read the words.

1. cane

2. pen

3. key

4. purse

5. bag

6. wallet

7. watch

8. book

9. credit card

10. umbrella

11. shopping bag

12. computer

Your Turn Use the words. Make your own conversations.

Skills Check

A **LISTEN** Task 1: Follow the directions. Choose the correct picture.
Task 2: You will hear five conversations. Choose the correct picture.

B **READ** Read the five conversations below. Choose the correct picture.

1 Hi, Jack.
Hi, Mary. How are you?
Fine, thanks.

2 Good morning, Ken.
Good morning, Dan. This is a new student, Sally Green.
Hi, Sally. Nice to meet you.
Nice to meet *you*.

3 —So long, Sue.
—Bye, Jim. See you tomorrow.

4 Is his name Fred Brown?
No, it is not.
Well, what is it?
It's Fred Burns.

5 —Is this train on Track Nine?
—No, it's on Track Three.

C **WRITE** Choose pictures and write your own conversations.

D **ROLE-PLAY** Act out your conversations.

② THE CLOTHING STORE

Listen first.
Then talk about the picture.

1. boots
2. scarves
3. nightgowns
4. bathing suits
5. bathrobes
6. shorts
7. jackets
8. blouses
9. shoes
10. jeans

Excuse me. Where are the **shoes**?

They are in **Department Two.**

1

Listen first. Practice the model conversations.

What is your favorite color? It is **blue.**

brown   white   red   black   green

orange   purple   gray   yellow   blue

Make new conversations.

What color is your new **scarf?**  It is **blue.**

1.

2.

3.

4.

Identifying colors
20   To be: *is/are*

Listen first. Practice the model sentences. Make new sentences.

What color are your new **shoes**?

They are **brown.**

1. slacks

2. shorts

3. socks

4. boots

5. slippers

6. jeans

7. glasses

8. gloves

9. sandals

Listen first. Practice the model conversation.
Make new conversations.

1. a yellow scarf

2. a red blouse

3. a black suit

4. a purple hat

5. a white jacket

6. a blue skirt

Listen first. Practice the model conversation.
Make new conversations.

What's Carla wearing?

He's wearing **gray slacks.**

She's wearing **orange shorts.**
What's Peter wearing?

1. green socks

2. black boots

3. gray jeans

4. red sunglasses

5. blue slippers

6. pink gloves

Your Turn   **What are your friends wearing? What are you wearing?**

Listen first. Ask and answer the questions.

1. Who is wearing a brown sweater?   Frank is.

2. Who is wearing gray slacks?   Peter is.

3. Is Patty wearing a green dress?   Yes, she is.

4. Is Carla wearing orange shoes?   No, she is not.

5. Is Peter wearing gray slacks   He is wearing gray slacks.
   or gray jeans?

6. Is Frank wearing a brown sweater   He is wearing a brown
   or a brown hat?   sweater.

Describing what people are wearing
24   Present progressive

Listen first. Ask and answer the questions.

What is he doing?   He is singing.

1. What is she doing?      She is reading.

2. What is he doing?      He is eating.

3. What is she doing?      She is eating.

4. What is he doing?      He is cooking.

5. What are they doing?      They are listening to music.

6. What are they doing?      They are playing a video game.

7. What are they doing?      They are watching TV.

8. What are they doing?      They are drinking coffee.

Listen first. Practice the model conversation.
Make new conversations.

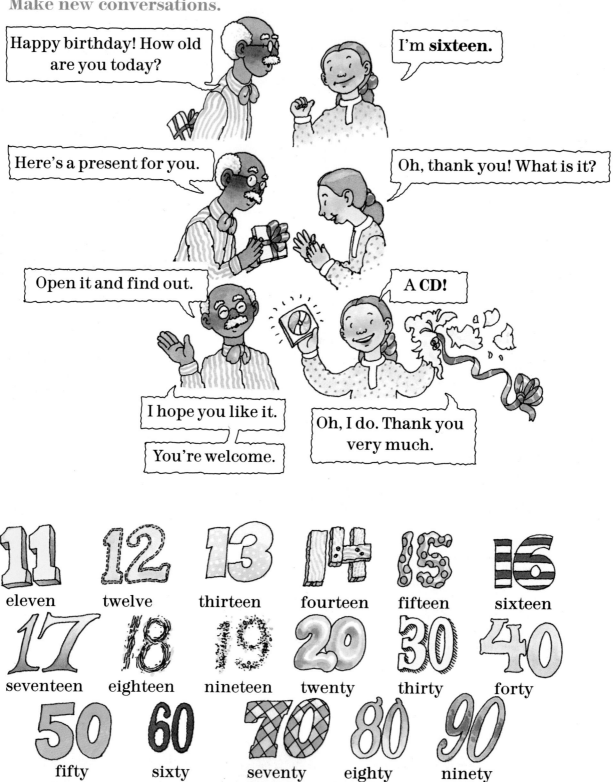

Happy birthday! How old are you today?

I'm **sixteen.**

Here's a present for you.

Oh, thank you! What is it?

Open it and find out.

A **CD!**

I hope you like it.

You're welcome.

Oh, I do. Thank you very much.

11 eleven	12 twelve	13 thirteen	14 fourteen	15 fifteen	16 sixteen
17 seventeen	18 eighteen	19 nineteen	20 twenty	30 thirty	40 forty
50 fifty	60 sixty	70 seventy	80 eighty	90 ninety	

Using numbers 11-20

Useful Words

Listen first. Then listen again and read the words.

1. CD

2. necklace

3. bracelet

4. tape

5. doll

6. backpack

7. puzzle

8. camera

9. ring

10. T-shirt

11. basketball

12. tennis racquet

Your Turn   Use the words. Make your own conversations.

Skills Check

A LISTEN Task 1: Follow the directions. Choose the correct picture.
Task 2: You will hear five conversations. Choose the correct picture.

B READ Read the five conversations below. Choose the correct picture.

1 —I like your red coat.
—Thanks, and I like your blue hat!

2 Anita is not happy with her new jeans.
Why not?
She doesn't like purple.

3 What are you wearing?
I'm wearing my white dress. What is Liz wearing?
She's wearing a gray skirt.

4 Is he playing?
No, he isn't.
Well, what is he doing?
He's eating his lunch.

5 Today is my birthday.
How old are you?
I'm ninety years old.
That's great! Did you get any presents?
Yes, I got a bracelet from my grandchildren.

C WRITE Choose pictures and write your own conversations.

D ROLE-PLAY Act out your conversations.

3

AT HOME

Listen first.
Then talk about the picture.

1. kitchen

2. living room

3. bedroom

4. bathroom

5. hall

6. basement

7. yard

8. closet

9. laundry room

10. driveway

Where's my **sweatshirt?**

It's in the **bedroom.**

Vocabulary building
Asking for and giving information

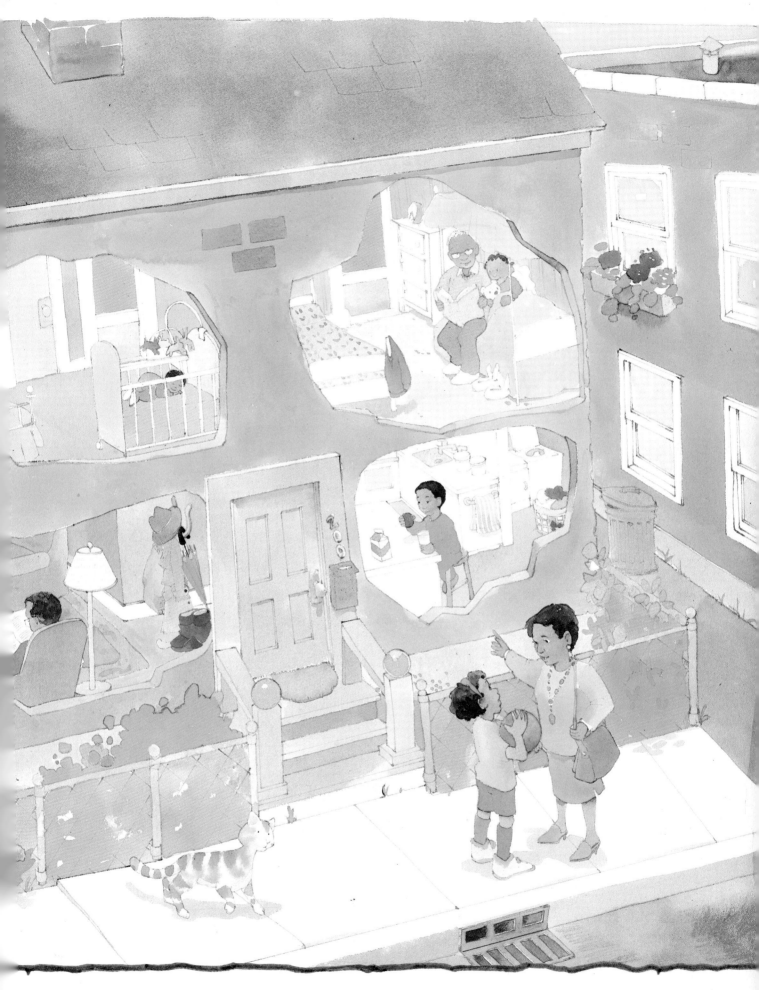

Listen first. Ask and answer the questions.

1. Where is my tie?  It is on the bookcase.

2. Where is my hat?  It is on the rug.

3. Where is my belt?  It is under the chair.

4. Where is my shirt?  It is under the table.

5. Where is my raincoat?  It is on the floor.

6. Where is my towel?  It is under the sink.

7. Where is my brush?  It is on the bureau.

8. Where is my sweater?  It is on the couch.

Talking about locations
Prepositions: *on/under*

Listen first. Practice asking and answering the questions.

Rosa is in the bathroom. Her towel is on the toilet. Her brush is on the shelf. Her bathrobe is on the mirror. Her glasses are on the sink. Her slippers are on the rug.

1. Where is her towel?	It is on the toilet.
2. Where is her brush?	It is on the shelf.
3. Where is her bathrobe?	It is on the mirror.
4. Where are her glasses?	They are on the sink.
5. Where are her slippers?	They are on the rug.

Listen first. Ask and answer the questions.

Bill is in the kitchen. His shirt is on the counter. His jacket is under the chair. His belt is on the refrigerator. His socks are on the stove. His shoes are under the table.

1. What is on the counter?

2. What is under the chair?

3. What is on the refrigerator?

4. What is on the stove?

5. What is under the table?

Listen first. Practice the model conversations.

1. What time is it?
   It's ten-fifteen.
   Ten-thirty?
   No, *ten-fifteen.*

2. What time is it?
   It's ten-thirty.
   Eleven-thirty?
   No, *ten-thirty.*

3. What time is it?
   It's ten-twenty.
   Nine-twenty?
   No, *ten-twenty.*

4. What time is it?
   It's ten forty-five.
   Ten-fifteen?
   No, *ten forty-five.*

Make new conversations.

Hurry, it's late!
   What time is it?
It's **ten-twenty.**
   No, it isn't. It's only **nine-thirty.** It's early.

1.

2.

3.

4.

Listen first. Practice the model conversations.

Hi, Mom.
What are you doing?

Seven in the morning, or seven in the evening?

Okay. Bye for now.
Love you.

Hi, Richard.
I'm making a shopping list.
Call me tomorrow at seven.

In the evening.

Bye. Love you too.

Make new conversations.

1. 9:00
   in the morning/at night
   In the morning.

2. 5:00
   in the morning/in the afternoon
   In the afternoon.

3. 12:00
   at noon/at midnight
   At noon.

4. 6:00
   in the morning/in the evening
   In the evening.

Time phrases *in the morning/evening/at night*
Creating new conversations   **35**

GRAMMAR PRACTICE

2

Listen first. Practice the model sentences. Make new sentences.

1. Is Tom in the car?  No, he is not. He is *under* the car!

2. Are the children behind the door?  No, they are not. They are *in front of* the door!

3. Is Clara under the couch?  No, she is not. She is *on* the couch!

4. Are you in the bathroom?  No, I am not. I am in the *bedroom!*

5. Are you two on the rug?  No, we are not. We are *under* the rug!

1.

2.

3.

4.

Talking about locations

Prepositions: *on/under/in front of*

Listen first. Read the sentences.

1. The baby is in front of the man.
   The man is behind the baby.

2. The man is in front of the woman.
   The woman is behind the man.

3. The woman is in front of the little girl.
   The little girl is behind the woman.

4. The little girl is in front of the old man.
   The old man is behind the little girl.

Look at the picture. Make new sentences.

Listen first. Practice the model conversations.

Fare, please.

No, You're on the wrong bus.
You want bus number **83.**

You're welcome.

Is this the bus
for the **library?**

Thanks.

Is this the bus for the **train station?**

Yes, it is.

Taking public transportation
Roleplaying conversations

Useful Words

Listen first. Then listen again and read the words.

1. university

2. airport

3. football stadium

4. bank

5. supermarket

6. hospital

7. police station

8. post office

9. TV station

10. mall

11. high school

12. library

Your Turn　**Use the words. Make your own conversations.**

Skills Check

A LISTEN Task 1: Follow the directions. Choose the correct picture.
Task 2: You will hear five conversations. Choose the
correct picture.

B READ Read the five conversations below. Choose the correct picture.

1 —Where is my raincoat?
—It's on the floor.

2 Where is Martin's hat?
It's on the table.
Where are his boots?
They are in the closet.

3 Wake up, Roberto!
What time is it?
It's ten-fifteen.
Ten-fifteen in the evening?
No! In the morning!

4 Where is the cat?
It's under the bed.
On the bed?
No, *under* the bed!

5 I'm waiting for you at the library.
Inside the library?
No, *in front of* the library.

C WRITE Choose pictures and write your own conversations.

D ROLE-PLAY Act out your conversations.

4 AT THE OFFICE

Listen first.
Then talk about the picture.

1. pay phone
2. first aid kit
3. copy machine
4. computer
5. fax machine
6. coffee machine
7. ladies' room
8. men's room
9. elevator
10. stairwell

Vocabulary building
Asking for and giving locations

WOMEN MEN PHONE FAX ELEVATOR STAIRWELL FIRST AID

Listen first. Practice the conversations.

1. Who is this girl?
       It is my daughter.
   What color is her hair?
       It is black.
   Is she thin or heavy?
       She is heavy.
   And what color are her eyes?
       They are black.

2. Who is this boy?
       It is my son.
   What color is his hair?
       It is blond.
   Is he tall or short?
       He is short.
   And what color are his eyes?
       They are brown.

3. Who is this man?
       It is my husband.
   What color is his hair?
       It is red.
   What color are his eyes?
       They are blue.
   Is he thin or fat?
       He is thin.

4. Who is this woman?
       It is my wife.
   What color is her hair?
       It is brown.
   What color are her eyes?
       They are green.
   Is she tall or short?
       She is tall.

Your Turn   **Describe someone in your family.**

Listen first. Practice the model conversation.
Make new conversations.

Who is that **woman** over there?
    Where?
There — the **tall woman in the red dress.**
    Oh, that is **Gina.**
What is her last name?
    It is **Papa.**

1. Sam/Kirk

2. Tim/Lang

Listen first. Practice the conversations.

Look, this is Ted.
    Is he your new boyfriend?
Yes, he is.
    What is he like?
Well, he is thin. His hair is red, and
his eyes are green. He is very tall and
handsome. And he is twenty-four.

Look, this is Kate.
    Is she your new girlfriend?
Yes, she is.
    What is she like?
Well, she is short. Her hair is blond,
and her eyes are blue. She is
thirty-one and very pretty!

Listen first. Practice the model conversation.
Make new conversations.

Operator. May I help you?

Jim Bennett, please.

Benny?

No, Bennett.

Can you spell that, please?

B-E-N-N-E-T-T

Thank you. That's extension **9440.**

9040?

No, **9440.**

ABCDEFGHIJKLM
NOPQRSTUVWXYZ

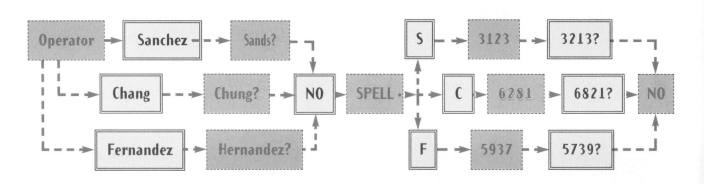

Operator → Sanchez --→ Sands?

Chang --→ Chung? --→ NO → SPELL

Fernandez → Hernandez?

S → 3123 → 3213?

C → 6281 → 6821? → NO

F → 5937 → 5739?

Listen first. Practice the model conversation.
Make new conversations.

Can I help you?

Your name?

Can you spell your last name, please?

And your address?

And the zip?

01938?

Thank you.

Yes. Please send your new catalog.

Jill Foster

F-O-S-T-E-R

4631 Fairfield Avenue, Missoula, Montana

01948

No, 01948.

1. Joshua Lubar
   99 Banks Street
   Buffalo, New York 10606

2. Sandra Franco
   112 West Fort Lee Road
   Hoboken, New Jersey 07603

3. Susan Gordon
   525 West Street
   Houston, Texas 77069

4. Max Dugan
   6624 Partin Place
   Orlando, Florida 32812

5. Sabina Ward
   1431 Brett Place
   San Pedros, California 90732

Listen first. Practice the model sentences. Make new sentences.

What is Calvin doing?   He is **typing**.

1. filing

2. talking on the phone

3. drawing

4. working at the computer

5. sending a fax

6. delivering the mail

Talking about office duties
Present progressive

Listen first. Practice the model conversation.
Make new conversations.

Where is Sylvia?
What is she doing?

She's **at the gas station.**
She is **buying gas.**

1. at the travel agency
   buying tickets

2. at the post office
   buying stamps

3. at the drugstore
   buying sunglasses

4. at the deli
   buying sandwiches

5. at the shoe store
   buying boots

6. at the newsstand
   buying magazines

Can I help you?

It's **fifty cents.**

It's **a dollar.**

Thank you.
And here's your change.

How much is this **pen?**

And how much is this **book?**

Here **are two dollars.**

Thank you. Bye.

cents   dollars   a penny   a nickel

a dime   a quarter   a dollar bill   a five-dollar bill

Useful Words

Listen first. Then listen again and read the words.

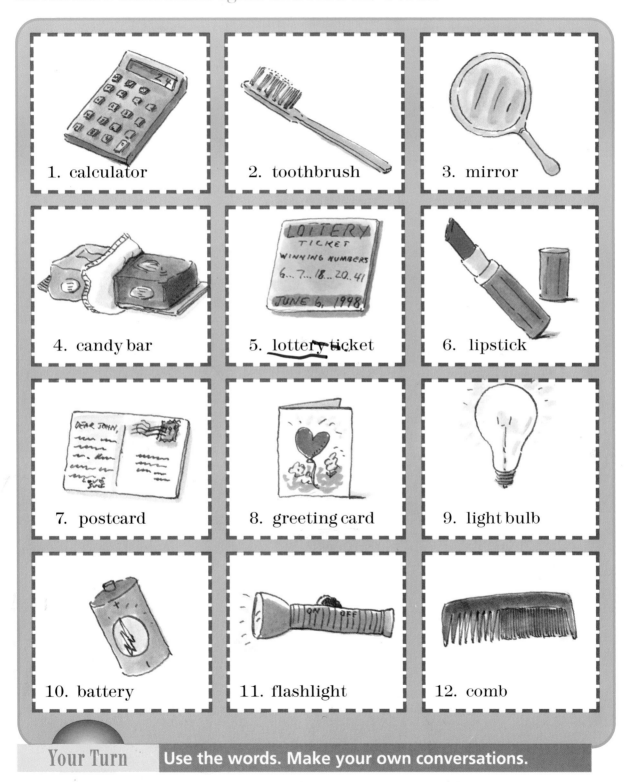

1. calculator

2. toothbrush

3. mirror

4. candy bar

5. lottery ticket

6. lipstick

7. postcard

8. greeting card

9. light bulb

10. battery

11. flashlight

12. comb

Your Turn Use the words. Make your own conversations.

Skills Check

A **LISTEN** Task 1: Follow the directions. Choose the correct picture.
Task 2: You will hear five conversations. Choose the
correct picture.

B **READ** Read the five conversations below. Choose the correct picture.

1 —Where's the copy machine?
—It's next to the stairwell.

2 Who is that woman talking on the phone?
The heavy woman with brown hair?
Yes.
She's my wife.

3 Is Mr. Wang in?
I'm sorry. He's not. Who is calling, please?
Maria Bowker.
Please spell your last name.
B-O-W-K-E-R
What's your phone number?
863-2247
I'll give Mr. Wang the message.
Thank you.

4 Where is your father?
He's at the deli.
What is he doing?
He's buying sandwiches.

5 How much is a lottery ticket?
One dollar.
I'll take two. Here are two dollars.
And here are your tickets. Good luck!

C **WRITE** Choose pictures and write your own conversations.

D **ROLE-PLAY** Act out your conversations.

IN THE KITCHEN

Listen first.
Then talk about the picture.

1. silverware

2. mop

3. broom

4. pots and pans

5. dishes

6. vacuum cleaner

7. garbage can

8. glasses

9. cabinet

10. dustpan

Where is the silverware?

In the drawer.

Where are the glasses?

On the shelf.

Vocabulary building
Asking for and giving location

Listen first. Practice the model sentences.

1. What is he eating?   He is eating a <u>carrot</u>.

2. What is he eating?   He is eating a banana.

3. What is he eating?   He is eating a sandwich.

4. What is he eating?   He is eating an apple.

5. What is he eating?   He is eating an egg.

6. What is he eating?   He is eating an orange.

What is he eating? Make new sentences.

1.   2.   3.

4.   5.   6.

Identifying foods
56   Present progressive: *eating*

Listen first. Practice the model sentences.

She is buying a banana.

She is buying sandwiches.

She is buying an apple.

She is buying grapes.

What is she buying? Make new sentences.

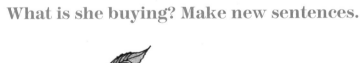

1.

2.

3.

4.

5.

6.

CONVERSATION PRACTICE ①

Listen first. Practice the model conversation.

Listen first. Practice the model conversation.
Make your own conversations.

Can you meet me later?

At about **four o'clock.**

At the park.

Bye.

What time?

Sure. Where?

Fine. See you later.

1. beach

2. coffee shop

3. fish pond

4. gym

5. playground

6. swimming pool

7. community center

8. bookstore

9. zoo

10. park

11. lake

12. toy store

Listen first. Ask and answer the questions.

1. What is he drinking?  He is drinking coffee.

2. What is she drinking?  She is drinking water.

3. What is she drinking?  She is drinking lemonade.

4. What is he drinking?  He is drinking tea.

1. What is she eating?  She is eating bread.

2. What is he eating?  He is eating ice cream.

3. What is he eating?  He is eating pizza.

4. What is she eating?  She is eating cheese.

Listen first. Ask and answer the questions.

1. What is he doing?
   What is he **drinking?**

   He is **drinking.**
   He is **drinking milk.**

2. What is she doing?
   What is she **eating?**

   She is **eating.**
   She is **eating fish.**

Make new questions and answers.

1.

2.

3.

4.

Listen first. Practice the model conversation.

Making polite requests
Roleplaying conversations

Useful Words

Listen first. Then listen again and read the words.

1. spaghetti

2. salad

3. chicken

4. fruit

5. salt

6. soup

7. sugar

8. pepper

9. napkin

10. spoon

11. knife

12. fork

Your Turn Use the words. Make your own conversations.

Skills Check

A **LISTEN** Task 1: Follow the directions. Choose the correct picture.
Task 2: You will hear five conversations. Choose the correct picture.

B **READ** Read the five conversations below. Choose the correct picture.

1 Where is the broom?
It's in the closet.
And where is the dustpan?
It's on the shelf.

2 What is she eating?
She's eating an apple.
What is he eating?
He's eating a sandwich.

3 Let's go to the playground.
What time?
At 3:15.
Sounds great. See you then!

4 Where is Gabe?
He's at the swimming pool.
Is he swimming?
No. He's eating ice cream.

5 Please eat your soup.
I need a spoon.
Here's a spoon for you.
Thank you.
You're welcome.

C **WRITE** Choose pictures and write your own conversations.

D **ROLE-PLAY** Act out your conversations.

THE COMMUNITY CENTER

Listen first.
Then talk about the picture.

1. cook
2. electrician
3. advertising assistant
4. X-ray technician
5. computer programmer
6. security guard
7. teacher
8. cashier
9. salesclerk
10. mechanic

Anything interesting on the job board?

Yes—here's a job for **a cook.**

ELECTRICIAN
AVERY CONSTRUCTION
356-1165

ADVERTISING ASSISTANT
BAY CITY NEWS
WED. THURS. FRI.
TELEPHONE SALES
CALL THE PAPER
221-8100
ASK FOR TED

COOK- FULL TIME
225-2110
PHIL'S DINER...
MAIN STREET
START NOW !!

COMPUTER
PROGRAMMER
COMMUNITY COLLEGE
GOOD SALARY
Call - 414-8743

SECURITY
GUARD
SALTY BEACH PARK
Weeknights
11 P.M. to 6 A.M.
811-0023

X RAY TECHNICIAN
Medical Center
expeience Required
482-3346

Teacher
Summer School
Grades 9-10
Call
212-655-1478

Cashier
Sloan's
Supermarket
Weekends 8-4
$5/hr.

CLERK
Walker Shoes
Evenings 6-9
Apply at store
208 Main Street

AUTO
MECHANICS
NEEDED
Auto Parts
International
Call 332-5353

Listen first. Practice the model sentences. Make new sentences.

Are you still **a secretary?**

No, I am **an executive** now.

1. flight attendant   pilot   2. nurse   doctor

3. taxi driver   lawyer   4. engineer   architect

5. accountant   army officer   6. waiter   musician

Listen first. Ask and answer the questions.
Make new questions and answers.

1. Are you American? No, I am not.
   Are you Mexican? No, I am not.
   Are you Columbian? Yes, I am.

2. Are you twenty-six? No, I am not.
   Are you nineteen? Yes, I am.

3. Are you a taxi driver? No, I am not.
   Are you a student? Yes, I am.

4. You're Anita Ramos! That is right.

Haitian 24 engineer Marie Decou	Canadian 28 accountant Alex Osborne	American 36 cook Gilbert Muller	Vietnamese 44 teacher Hung Phan
Japanese 32 cashier Yoshio Ono	Hmong 21 nurse Joua Vang	Cambodian 57 doctor Dr. Chunn	Chinese 64 teacher Vivian Wan
Mexican 32 secretary Marta Sanchez	Russian 19 musician Rada Nijinska	Brazilian 29 security guard Eduardo Amos	American 41 taxi driver Ken Pratt
Brazilian 27 army officer Julio Branco	Mexican 19 flight attendant Delsa Gonzalez	Korean 39 cook Kwon June	Vietnamese 51 cashier Tung Phan
Korean 70 architect Yong Yeon Park	Puerto Rican 19 student Anita Ramos	Chinese 80 waiter Ming Pei	Japanese 25 teacher Setsuko Toyama

CONVERSATION PRACTICE

1

Listen first. Practice the model conversation.

Good morning.
   Good morning. What's your name, please?
My name is **Jane Marshall.**
   Are you **Canadian?**
Yes, I am.
   How old are you?
I'm **forty-six.**
   And what's your occupation?
I'm a **doctor.**
   How long are you staying?
Two weeks.
   Thank you. That's all.
Thank *you.* Good-bye.

Giving personal information
70   Roleplaying conversations

Make new conversations.

Pat Putnam	American	42	doctor
Boris Renko	Russian	53	actor
John Cooper	English	39	football player
Maria Tiant	Puerto Rican	29	author
Miguel Pinto	Venezuelan	60	plumber
Carol Chen	Taiwanese	72	waitress

Listen first. Ask and answer the questions.

1. How many passengers are there?   There are nine passengers.

2. How many suitcases are there?   There are six suitcases.

3. How many newspapers are there?   There are four newspapers.

4. How many books are there?   There is one book.

5. How many umbrellas are there?   There is one umbrella.

6. How many chairs are there?   There are eight chairs.

7. How many computers are there?   There is one computer.

8. How many cassette players are there?   There is one cassette player.

Asking for and giving information
There is/There are

Bay City is a small town in the United States. It is not far from Boston. It is on the ocean. There are five trains to Boston every morning, but there is only one bus.

Main Street is in the middle of Bay City. There are many buildings and stores on Main Street. There is City Hall, the post office, and the parking garage. There is a new mall. There are thirteen stores inside the mall. There is a big clock tower outside the mall.

On High Street there is a community center. There is a bus stop behind the community center.

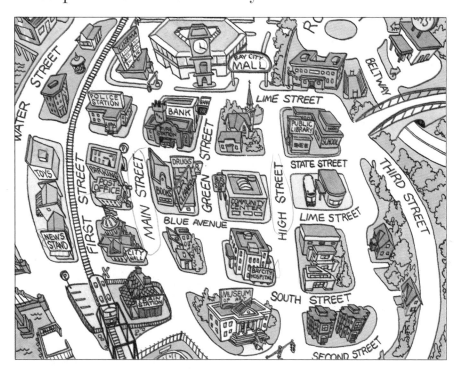

1. How many trains to Boston are there?

2. How many hospitals are there?

3. How many buses are there every morning?

4. Is there one post office or are there two post offices?

5. Is there one community center or are there two community centers?

6. What else can you say about Bay City?

Ask and answer more questions about Bay City.

Listen first. Practice the model conversation.
Make new conversations.

Something's wrong with the **toilet!** Call the **plumber.**

I don't know.

Uhh, **Elliott Plumbing,** I think.

What's the number?

What's the name?

Here it is—**556-7076.**

1. TV/repairman

2. car/mechanic

3. lights/electrician

4. roof/roofer

5. stairs/carpenter

6. sink/plumber

Useful Words

▶ Carpenters

Brodie, Joyce ---------------------------- 264-9930

SANTIAGO AND SANTIAGO
Experienced Carpenters
--- 355-9560

SMITH, BRUCE
Carpentry and Woodworking
--- 760-7067

▶ Electricians

Alice A. Anderson
AAA ELECTRICIANS
--- 443-8495

Howse, Brad
Master Electrician --------------------955-1234

KANG, CHONG -------------------------- 369-9701

▶ Mechanics

MUNDAHL MECHANICS
John Mundahl,
Owner/Operator ---------------------- 554-6167

Nunez, Victor ------------------------------ 485-5894

TAMM, PETER
Licensed Mechanic ----------------- 324-3434

▶ Plumbers

DICK ELLIOTT PLUMBING AND HEATING
--- 556-7076

Gibbons Brothers Plumbers-------- 887-9090

Ricardo, Juan --------------------------- 996-0768

▶ Roofers

Sakamura, Ichiro ---------------------- 665-7595

SILVA AND SONS ROOFERS
Call toll free: ----------------- 1-800-270-9543

THORNTON, MARTHA
Roofing Contractor ----------------- 336-8670

▶ TV Repair

CHANG'S TV
Kim Chang,
Master Technician
--- 875-2306

RIVERA'S REPAIR SERVICE
TVs & VCRs
--- 562-1731

Van Stone, Pam ------------------------- 266-4766

 Your Turn | Use the ads. Make your own conversations.

Skills Check

A LISTEN Task 1: Follow the directions. Choose the correct picture.
Task 2: You will hear five conversations. Choose the
correct picture.

B READ Read the five conversations below. Choose the correct picture.

1 —What is your occupation?
—I'm an army officer.

2 What is your name?
    Maria Ortiz.
How old are you?
    I'm 32.
What is your occupation?
    I'm a musician.

3 How many suitcases are there?
    There are two suitcases.
And how many umbrellas are there?
    There is one umbrella.

4 How many banks are there?
    There is one bank.
Where is it?
    It's next to the post office.

5 —What's wrong with the light?
—I don't know, but the electrician is fixing it.

C WRITE Choose pictures and write your own conversations.

D ROLE-PLAY Act out your conversations.

FAMILY REUNION

Listen first.
Then talk about the picture.

1. dancing
2. playing tennis
3. riding a bike
4. playing catch
5. playing the guitar
6. chasing the _____
7. emptying the trash
8. laughing
9. telling jokes
10. taking pictures

What's **Charlie** doing?

He's **taking pictures.**

Vocabulary building
Asking for and giving information

Listen first. Read the story. Ask and answer the questions.

The Gonzalez Family

The Parents		The Children	
Rose Gonzalez	Louis Gonzalez	Jim Gonzalez	Gina Gonzalez
mother	father	son	daughter
wife	husband	brother	sister
48	45	15	21

I'm Rose Gonzalez. I'm a housewife. My husband's name is Louis. He's a plumber. I'm forty-eight years old. Louis is forty-five. Jim is my son. He's fifteen. Gina is my daughter. She's twenty-one. Jim is still a student. Gina is an artist.

1. Who is Jim's father?   Louis Gonzalez is.

2. Who is Jim's sister?   Gina is.

3. Who is Louis's wife?   Rose Gonzalez is.

4. Who is Rose Gonzalez's son?   Jim is.

5. Who is a housewife?   Rose is.

6. Who is a plumber?   Louis is.

7. Who are the Gonzalez children? Jim and Gina are.

8. Who are Gina's parents?   Rose and Louis Gonzalez are.

Listen first. Practice the model conversations.

1. Are you eighteen?
   No, I am not.
   Are you nineteen?
   Yes, I am.

2. Are you mother and daughter?
   No, we are not.
   Are you grandmother and
   granddaughter?
   Yes, we are.

3. Are you husband and wife?
   No, we are not.
   Are you brother and sister?
   No, we are not.
   Well, are you father and
   daughter?
   Yes, we are.

4. Are they brother and sister?
   No, they are not.
   Are they husband and wife?
   No, they are not.
   Are they mother and son?
   Yes, they are.

5. Are you father and son?
   No, we are not.
   Are you brothers?
   No, we are not.
   Are you friends?
   Yes, we are. We are good
   friends.

6. Are you the grandfather?
   No, I am not.
   Are you the father?
   No, I am not.
   Well, what are you?
   I am the grandson!

Your Turn   **Make conversations about your family.**

Listen first. Practice the model conversations.
Make new conversations.

FEELING FINE	FEELING NOT SO FINE
I'm great!	Awful.
Never felt better!	Tired.
Just swell.	So, so.
Fabulous.	Oh, okay.
Very well, thank you.	Stressed out.
Good, really good.	Not good.

 Your Turn   **Ask your friends how they feel.**

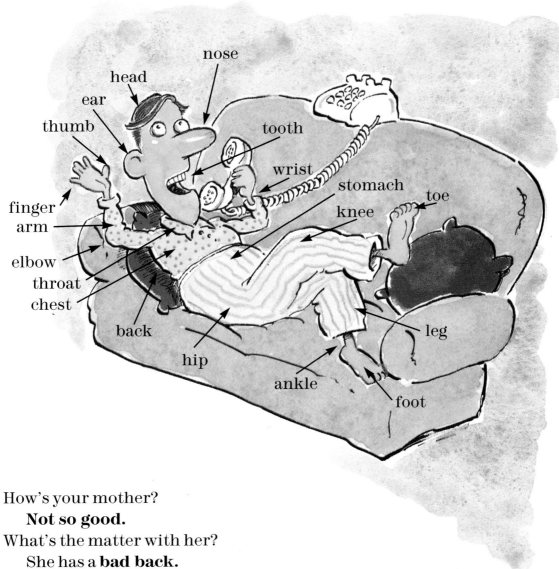

How's your mother?
   Not so good.
What's the matter with her?
   She has a **bad back.**
How is your father?
   Awful.
What's the matter with *him?*
   He has a **bad knee.**
Well, how are you?
   Terrible!
What's the matter with *you?*
   My **tooth** hurts.

Listen first. Ask and answer the questions.

1. Is she in the kitchen?
    What is she doing?

    Yes, she is.
    She is washing the dishes.

2. Is he in the bathroom?
    What is he doing?

    Yes, he is.
    He is taking a shower.

3. Are you in the living room?
    Where *are* you?
    What are you doing?

    No, I am not.
    I am in the laundry room.
    I am ironing.

4. Is she in the kitchen?
    Where *is* she?
    What is she doing?

    No, she is not.
    She is in the living room.
    She is listening to CDs.

5. Are they in the bedroom?
    Where *are* they?
    What are they doing?

    No, they are not.
    They are in the kitchen.
    They are making tea.

6. Are you two in the bedroom?
    Where *are* you?
    What are you doing?

    No, we are not.
    We are in the living room.
    We are watching a video.

Listen first. Read the story. Ask and answer the questions.

The Palmero family is at home. Bob Palmero is in the kitchen. He is cooking. Anita Palmero is in the living room. She is sitting in a recliner. She is reading a newspaper. Tommy Palmero and his friend, Jorge, are in the driveway. They are playing basketball. Rosita Palmero is in her bedroom. She and her friend Carol are working on the computer.

1. Is Mr. Palmero in the living room?

No, he is not.
He is in the kitchen.

2. Is Mrs. Palmero in the kitchen?

No, she is not.
She is in the living room.

3. Is Mrs. Palmero reading a book?

No, she is not.
She is reading a newspaper.

4. Are Tommy and Jorge in the kitchen?

No, they are not.
They are in the driveway.

5. Are they playing football?

No, they are not.
They are playing basketball.

6. Are Rosita and Carol in the kitchen?

No, they are not.
They are in Rosita's bedroom.

Listen first. Practice the model conversations.
Make new conversations.

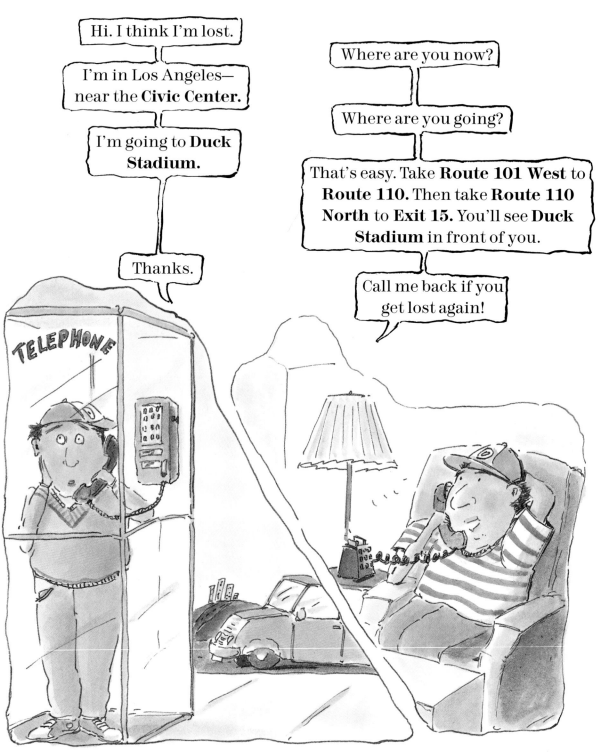

Hi. I think I'm lost.

I'm in Los Angeles— near the **Civic Center.**

I'm going to **Duck Stadium.**

Thanks.

Where are you now?

Where are you going?

That's easy. Take **Route 101 West** to **Route 110.** Then take **Route 110 North** to **Exit 15.** You'll see **Duck Stadium** in front of you.

Call me back if you get lost again!

Giving directions

Useful Words

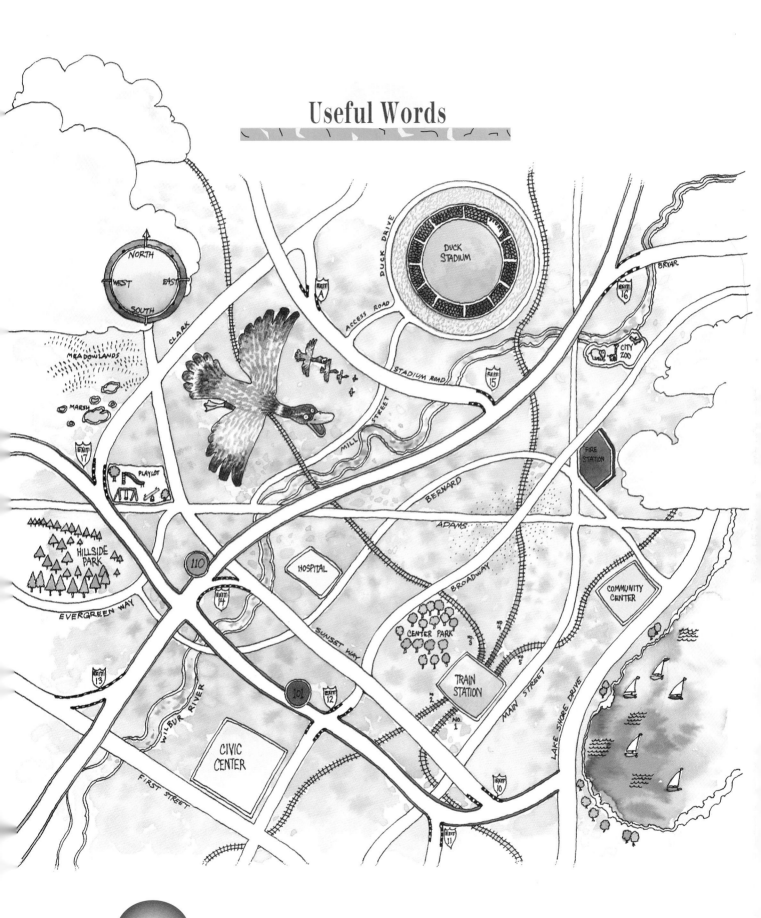

Skills Check

A **LISTEN** Task 1: Follow the directions. Choose the correct picture.
Task 2: You will hear five conversations. Choose the correct picture.

B **READ** Read the five conversations below. Choose the correct picture.

1 —What is Max doing?
—He's playing catch.

2 These are my sisters, Frances and Joanne.
How old are they?
Frances is 45 and Joanne is 36.
What do they do?
Frances is an artist. Joanne is a housewife and mother.

3 How are you?
I feel awful.
What's wrong?
I hurt my foot.

4 Where are your grandchildren?
They are in the living room.
What are they doing?
One is listening to CDs and the other is reading.

5 How do I get to Concord Road?
Get off at Exit 10 and turn right on Route 2.
What do I do next?
Just watch for Concord Road on the right.

C **WRITE** Choose pictures and write your own conversations.

D **ROLE-PLAY** Act out your conversations.

8
ON THE PHONE

Listen first.
Then talk about the picture.

1. dry cleaners
2. car wash
3. hardware store
4. hairdresser
5. barbershop
6. laundromat
7. gas station
8. office building
9. drugstore
10. fire station

> Which phone is nearest to the **dry cleaners?**

> The one **next to the car wash.**

Vocabulary building
Asking for and giving information

Listen first. Ask for and give directions.

1. —Excuse me. Where is the post office?
   —Go straight down Main Street for two blocks. It is on the right.

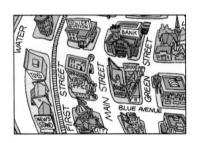

2. —Are there any good restaurants nearby?
   —Yes, there are. Cross First Street. Take a right on Water Street. The White Rainbow is on the left.

3. —Is it far to the library?
   —No. Take your first left on High Street and go two blocks. It is on the right-hand corner.

4. —Can you tell me where the Big Burger is?
   —Sure. Take the expressway to Exit 12. Go around the rotary to the Beltway. Big Burger is right behind the new mall.

1st 2nd 3rd

first   second   third

4th 5th

fourth   fifth

Look at the map. Ask for and give directions.

1. From the motel to the bookstore.
2. From the post office to the bus stop.
3. From the drugstore to the bank.
4. From the bus stop to the police station.

5. From the school to the museum.
6. From the zoo to the school.
7. From the train station to the library.
8. From the ferry to the hospital.

Listen first. Practice the model conversation.

Mainframe Computers.

Good morning.
My name is **Gail Simon.**

Good morning.
What can I do for you?

I'm calling about the
advertisement in the newspaper.

Which ad?

The one for a **computer
programmer.**

Your name again, please?

Simon. Gail Simon.

And your address,
Ms. Simon?

**495 Frement Avenue,
Houston, Texas 77059.**

Fine. I'll send you an application.
Thank you for calling.

Thank you.

Inquiring about a job
Roleplaying conversations

Choose any people. Choose any ads. Make new conversations.

The People

1. Charles Snow
   123 Chestnut Street
   Albany, New York 14224

2. Kim Goldberg
   15 West Avenue
   Houston, Texas 77069

3. Mary Ford
   826 South Lane
   Redwood City, California 94065

4. Don Freeman
   4525 Henry Hudson Parkway
   Bronx, New York 10471

5. Judy Morton
   365 Elm Street
   Highland Park, Illinois 60035

6. Terry Flores
   5 Green Court
   Miami, Florida 33186

7. Walter Masuda
   94 Sunset Place
   Honolulu, Hawaii 96797

The Ads

Cook
Phil's Diner
Evenings, some weekends
969-5055

Electrician
AAA Electronics
Must have master license
889-2345

Security Guard
Bay Bank
Competitive salary and benefits
Call days, 757-0393

Computer Programmer
Mainframe Computers
3-5 years experience required
595-3329, extension 75

X-ray Technician
Bay City Hospital
Full time
545-8686, extension 2478

Cashier
Will train
Stow Mini-Mart
263-8875

Mechanic
Mike's Motors
Knowledge of foreign cars a plus
929-4976

Teacher
ESL and Bilingual Classes
Neighborhood High School
Ask for Mr. Rogers
566-8768

Clerk
Weekends only
The Corner Store
774-0293

Listen first. Practice the model conversation.
Make new conversations.

When is your **party?**

What time?

SUNDAY
6:45 P.M.
PARTY

On **Sunday.**

At **6:45.**

MONDAY
1:00 P.M.
HAIRDRESSER APPOINTMENT

3:30 P.M.
JOB INTERVIEW

TUESDAY
NOON
LUNCH MEETING

6:45 P.M.
MUSIC LESSON

WEDNESDAY
10:00 AM.
DOCTOR'S APPOINTMENT

THURSDAY
9:45 A.M.
CHECK-UP

4:00 P.M.
ART CLASS

FRIDAY
5:00 P.M.
EYE TEST

8:00 PM.
BIRTHDAY PARTY

SATURDAY
2:00 PM.
DRIVER'S TEST

7:30 P.M.
DINNER
AT PHIL'S

Discussing appointments
Days of the week

Listen first. Practice the conversation.
Make new conversations.

When are you taking your vacation this year?

Oh, you are taking a **winter** vacation?

And where are you going?

In **January.**

Yes.

I am not sure.
Maybe to **Mexico.**

**Listen first. Practice the model conversation.
Make new conversations.**

sunny

windy

freezing

stormy

foggy

snowy

rainy

cloudy

warm

hot

cold

cool

Discussing the weather
Roleplaying conversations

Useful Words

Listen first. Then listen again and read the words.

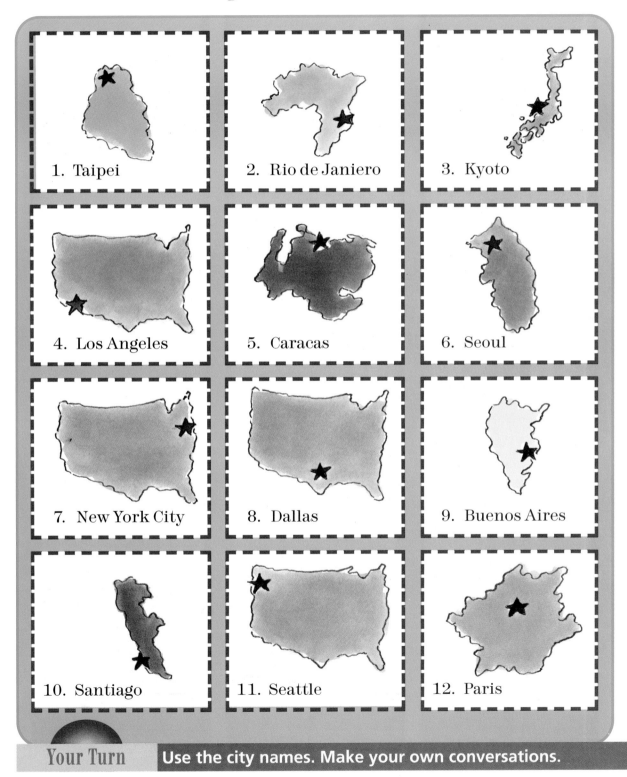

1. Taipei

2. Rio de Janiero

3. Kyoto

4. Los Angeles

5. Caracas

6. Seoul

7. New York City

8. Dallas

9. Buenos Aires

10. Santiago

11. Seattle

12. Paris

Your Turn   Use the city names. Make your own conversations.

Skills Check

A **LISTEN** Task 1: Follow the directions. Choose the correct picture.

Task 2: You will hear five conversations. Choose the correct picture.

B **READ** Read the five conversations below. Choose the correct picture.

Mail box.

1 —Where is the nearest bus stop?
—There is one on the corner, in front of the library.

2 Is that the new computer programmer?
Yes, it is. His name is Victor.
What's his last name?
García.
Where is he from?
He's from Mexico.

3 Can you come to the party on Saturday?
What time?
At 2:00.
Yes, but I have to leave early. I have a music lesson at 4:00.

4 When is your vacation this year?
In April.
Where are you going?
I'm going to Paris.
Paris in the spring! How wonderful!

5 Where are you?
I'm in Taipei.
What's the weather like?
It's rainy and windy.
Too bad. I think I'll stay here. It's hot and sunny.

C **WRITE** Choose pictures and write your own conversations.

D **ROLE-PLAY** Act out your conversations.

GRAMMAR SUMMARY

VERBS

SIMPLE PRESENT

to be (Units 1, 2, 3, 5, 8)
How **are** you?
His name **is** Bob.
Where **are** the shoes?
They **are** watching TV.
I **am** ninety years old.

there is/are (Unit 6)
There is one book.
There are eight chairs.

PRESENT PROGRESSIVE

is/are + ing
(Units 2, 4, 5, 7, 8)
He **is wearing** a brown
sweater.
She **is buying** a banana.
They **are watching** TV.

PRONOUNS

SUBJECT PRONOUNS

(Units 2, 4, 5, 6, 7)
I'm making a shopping list.
How old are **you?**
He/she is singing.
It is by the elevator.
No, **we** are not.
They are drinking coffee.

ADJECTIVES

COLORS

(Unit 2)
She is wearing a **green**
dress.

NATIONALITIES

(Unit 6)
Are you **American?**

POSSESSIVES

(Units 1, 2, 7)
Jim is **my** son.
What is **your** favorite color?
His name is Pete.
This is **her** sweater.

DEMONSTRATIVES

(Unit 1)
This is his shirt.
That is his tie.

ARTICLES

DEFINITE ARTICLE

the (Unit 2)
Where's **the** New York
train?

INDEFINITE ARTICLES

a and *an* (Units 5, 6)
Are you still **a** secretary?
No, I am **an** executive.

PREPOSITIONS

(Units 3, 8)
It's **in** the bedroom.
What is **on** the counter?
His jacket is **under** the
chair.
The baby is **in front of** the
man.

The little girls is **behind** the
woman.
The one **next to** the car
wash.
How do I get **from** the motel
to the bookstore?

QUESTIONS

QUESTION WORDS AND INFORMATION QUESTIONS

(Units 1, 2, 3, 4, 5, 6, 8)
Where are the shoes?
What is she doing?
Who is that woman?
When is your party?
How old are you today?
How much is this pen?
How many hospitals are
there?

INDEX

Communication and Vocabulary

Asking for and giving
directions 92-93
information 6, 18, 30, 66, 72, 78, 90
locations 19, 32, 36, 37, 42, 54
name and address 47
personal information 70
Arranging to meet 59

Describing
activities 85
community locations 83
family members 44-45
occupations/nationalities 71
ongoing activities 84
what people are doing 25, 61
what people are wearing 24
Dealing with an emergency 74
Using a map 87

Identifying
body parts 83
clothes 12, 13, 18, 19, 20, 21, 22, 23, 24, 31
colors 20
community places 39, 49, 59, 90, 91, 92, 93
days of the week 96
family members 80, 81
food, 56, 57, 60, 62, 63
kitchen equipment 54, 55
money 50
months/seasons of the year 97
occupations 66, 67, 68, 69, 70, 71, 74, 94, 95
office equipment 42, 43, 48
office locations/furnishings 43
personal belongings 14, 15, 27, 51
recreational activities 78, 79
rooms in a house 30, 31, 33, 36, 84
weather 98

Talking about
ages 81
appointments 96
community places 91
family members 80-81
health and feelings 82
jobs 68
names 8
occupations 67
office duties 48
parts of the body 83
recreation activities 79
shopping 49
vacations 97
work hours/salaries 67
Greetings/introductions/leavetakings 4, 5, 10, 58
Inquiring about a job 94
Making phone calls 46
Making polite requests 62
Taking public transportation 38
Telling time 34
Time phrases *in the morning/evening/at night* 35
Using colors to describe clothing 21, 23

Conversations
Creating new conversations 11, 15, 23, 27, 35, 39, 47, 51, 59, 63, 71, 75, 83, 87, 95, 99
Roleplaying conversations 10, 14, 17, 22, 26, 29, 34, 38, 41, 46, 50, 53, 58, 62, 65, 70, 74, 77, 82, 86, 89, 94, 99, 101
Writing conversations 17, 29, 41, 53, 65, 77, 89, 101

Grammar

Verbs
Present progressive 22, 24, 25, 48, 49, 56, 60, 61, 84
To be: *is/are* 20, 55
To be: *is/is not* 9
There is/There are 72, 73
Using action verbs 79

Pronouns
subject: *it, he, she, you, we, they*: 22, 25, 32, 36, 45, 48, 57, 60, 61, 62, 68, 69, 78, 81, 84

Adjectives
color 20, 21, 22, 23
descriptive 44, 45
nationality 69, 71
demonstrative: *this/that* 13, 50
possessive: *his/her* 8

Articles
a/an 57, 68

Prepositions
in 30, 33, 36
in front of/behind 36, 37
next to 90-91
on/under 32, 33, 36

Numbers
Using numbers 1-10: 7
Using numbers 11-20: 26
Using ordinals 92

Questions
Question word/information questions
what 9, 12
where 7, 43
Simple answers: *Yes, I am/No, I am not* 69

Listening Comprehension
16, 28, 40, 52, 64, 76, 88, 100

Reading Comprehension
16, 28, 33, 40, 52, 64, 73, 75, 76, 80, 85, 88, 95, 100

103

A Publication of The World Language Division

Contributing Writer/Product Development Director: Judith M. Bittinger

Executive Editor/Project Director: Elinor Chamas

Editorial Development: Elinor Chamas, Karen Howse, Clare Siska

Cover Design: Marshall Henrichs

Interior Design, Art Direction, and Production: AARTPACK, Inc.

Production/Manufacturing: James W. Gibbons

Illustrators: Elizabeth Allen 4-5, 30-31, 66-67; Len Ebert 8, 9, 25, 37, 44, 45, 62, 70, 80, 81; Charles Peale 14, 22, 23, 24, 34, 35, 48, 49, 60, 61, 74, 83, 98; John Sandford 10-11, 26, 36, 38, 56, 57, 68, 72, 84, 87, 96, 97; Rex Schneider 6-7, 42-43, 78-79; Dave Sullivan 17, 20, 21, 29, 32, 33, 41, 53, 65, 71, 73, 77, 82, 85, 89, 92, 93, 101; Laurie Sienkowski 18-19, 54-55, 90-91; Debbie Tilley 12, 13, 15, 27, 39, 46, 47, 50, 51, 58, 59, 63, 86, 94, 99.